Cool Cars!

Written by Emma Lynch

Let's check out some cool,
quick cars.

Have you ever seen one of them?
Is there one that you like best?

An Aston Martin is quick.

Speed: 0–62 in 4.8 seconds

Have you ever seen a Bond film? 007 has an Aston Martin car in six of the films.

One car has an ejector chair.
Bond can press a button to
shoot the chair out of the car!

A Ferrari is quicker.

Speed: 0–62 in 3.7 seconds

Ferraris are Italian sports cars.
They were track cars but now
they are road cars, too.

Have you ever seen this?
You can see one on the
bonnet of a Ferrari.

A Bugatti is quickest.

Speed: 0–62 in 2.5 seconds

Bugattis are French cars. This Bugatti is the quickest car – ever!

rubber

If you go at top speed for too long, then the rubber will start to melt!

What car is the quickest?
What car is in Bond films?
What car is Italian?